SABRINA FISHER REECE

Making More Money in Todays Market

For Those Who are Tired of Struggling Financially

In59Seconds Publishing Co

This book is for everyone who is open to learning how to change their relationship with money. Prosperity begins in the mind first. You were never meant to be poor. Let me teach you how I lived a life of Abundance when statistics said otherwise.

–SaBrina Fisher Reece

Contents

Preface

1

Money Mind

Before you make one new dollar this year, before you start a business, launch a side hustle, or create income that continues to flow long after the work is done, something far more important has to happen first. Your relationship with money has to change.

I want to be honest from the beginning. I have always expected money to be available to me. Not because life was perfect, not because doors magically opened, but because somewhere early on I believed that earning, creating, and increasing income was possible for me. That belief shaped my choices. I didn't grow up thinking there was a ceiling over my head. I never assumed there was a limit to what I could make. Even as a teenager, I hustled. I looked for opportunities. I expected results.

That mindset stayed with me. When I started my business in 1996, I hit the ground running. I didn't believe success was reserved for someone else or that prosperity was something I had to apologize for wanting. There was a brief season where I needed help, a single year where I relied on the system, and I am grateful that support existed. After that, I built my own business. Year after year, my income increased. Not overnight, I still had to advertise and market. It was not effortlessly. But I was consistent.

I understand that not everyone begins life with that expectation. Many people are taught to be cautious with money, to fear it, to feel undeserving of it, or to believe struggle is normal and prosperity is rare. If that was your experience, this book is for you. I am not here to judge where you started. I am here to show you that where you started does not have to determine where you end up.

Money is not just paper or numbers on a screen. It represents value. It moves as an exchange. When you solve a problem, provide a service, create something useful, save time, or improve someone's life, money is the return for that value. The issue is rarely ability. More often, it is belief, expectation, and focus.

Prosperity begins in the mind. When your thinking is aligned with growth, when your actions are consistent, and when you believe you are worthy of being compensated for what you bring to the table, money begins to move differently in your life. This book is about learning how to make that shift deliberately.

You do not need to come from money to build it. You do not need permission to want more. You do not need to struggle forever to prove your worth. You can learn to expect better. You can learn to focus differently. You can change your financial future within this lifetime.

That is why this book exists.

Every year brings new opportunities. We're in a time where ordinary people are becoming wealthy, not because they inherited money, or because they have special connections, but because they learned how to think differently. Wealth today is not limited to the educated, the privileged, or the lucky. It belongs to the people who dare to believe that abundance is available to them. It belongs to the people willing to learn, willing to evolve, and willing to break the poverty patterns of the past.

The truth is, money does not respond to desperation. It responds to clarity and confidence. It responds to a person who has made up their mind that they are worthy of wealth, deserving of overflow, and capable of learning whatever they need to learn to get to the next level. If you want this year to be a year of increase, you must first decide that you will no longer identify with struggle. Never speak the words "I am Broke" again.

Most of us were raised to believe that hard work alone creates success, but the real engine behind financial abundance is mental alignment. If you still feel unworthy deep inside, the money may come but it will slip through your fingers. If you fear failure, you'll sabotage opportunities before they ever take root. If you doubt your potential, you will talk yourself out of the very ideas that could change your life. That's why this book doesn't begin with "how to make money." It begins with **how to think like a person who attracts money.**

The new wealth mindset starts with understanding that money is not just paper, it is energy. It flows toward certainty, vision, and preparedness. It shows up for the person who already sees themselves winning. It responds to the person who treats their dreams with respect. Wealth does not come to the person waiting for things to get better. It comes to the person who decides, "This year, I am becoming better."

That is exactly what I did. This year, I started **#In59Seconds Publishing Co,** after owning a hair salon for thirty years. Braids, hair, and dreadlocks were all I knew. However, I became an author in 2018, and since then I have written fifteen best-selling self-help books. My first few books were published through a publishing company at a very high cost, and I eventually realized I didn't want to keep paying someone else to do what I could learn to do for myself. So a few years back, I decided it was time for me to figure this technology out—even though it was not my strong suit. It took three long months, staying up until midnight, but I did it. Not only did I publish my next five books, I taught myself how to do it for others, and I started a publishing company. The point is this: you can do anything. Even if it's a business you are not familiar with, learn it, master it, and then charge for it.

Residual income will not be optional, it will be necessary. The world has changed. Prices have changed. Opportunities have changed. But the greatest shift you can make is internal. Instead of saying, "I hope things work out," you must begin to say, "Everything I desire is already making its way to me." Instead of asking, "What if it doesn't work?" begin asking, "What if this is the year everything comes together?"

A new wealth mindset means you stop shrinking your dreams to match your income and start expanding your income to match your dreams. It means you stop apologizing for wanting more. You stop feeling guilty for wanting luxury, comfort, freedom, travel, or a better home. You stop believing that abundance is for other people. You start walking, speaking, planning, and preparing as if you expect overflow, not as if you're begging for scraps.

You cannot create new wealth with old thinking. You can't step into each new year carrying beliefs that belonged to 1999, 2005, or even last year. A wealthy mindset speaks differently. It sees differently. It expects differently. It looks at a closed door and says, "That's fine, I'll build my own." It looks at a setback and says, "This is temporary. Something better is coming." It looks at a new opportunity and doesn't ask, "Am I good enough?" It says, "I Am going to accomplish this."

The new wealth mindset requires you to become emotionally ready for abundance. You must be willing to release fear, release shame, release self-doubt, and release the limiting beliefs you inherited from people who did not know any better. Your parents and grandparents weren't wrong, they were uninformed. They weren't lacking ambition, they were lacking access and a vision of more. But *you* have access. You have tools. You have technology. You have knowledge at your fingertips that entire generations before you never had.

Now, you get to do what they could not do: you get to build wealth from your home. You get to create income without clocking in. COVID-19 created many opportunities for people to make tons of money and never leave their home. Now you get to design a life that doesn't drain you, but elevates you. There has never been a better time than right now to **capitalize on it**."

Everything begins with the decision to shift your thinking. Once your mindset changes, your behavior will follow. Once your behavior changes, your income will rise. Once your income rises, your lifestyle transforms. But the root of it all, the seed that everything else grows from, is the belief that you are capable of living a wealthier, freer, more abundant life.

This is your new beginning. This is your mental reset. I am excited for you. This is where your financial elevation truly starts. Because before you make more money this year, you must first become the version of you who can receive it, expect it, manage it, keep it and grow it.

Wealth begins in the mind. Abundance begins with belief. Your transformation begins now.

2

The Digital Age

There has never been a time in history where ordinary people had this much access, this much opportunity, and this much creative freedom. For generations, wealth was locked behind gates of education, privilege, location, and positions most of us were never invited into. You had to know the right people, be in the right place, or wait for someone to open a door for you. But the digital world changed everything. It leveled the playing field. It removed the gate and quietly handed the keys to anyone willing to learn, create, and show up.

Today, you do not need permission to prosper. You do not need approval to create. You do not need credentials to publish. You do not need investors to get started. What you need now is clarity, consistency, and the courage to finally transform your gifts into income. This era rewards people who are willing to stop waiting and start building.

Then COVID happened, and the world shifted in a way no one could have predicted. Offices shut down. Commutes disappeared overnight. Dining room tables became desks. Living rooms became studios. Kitchens became classrooms. And for the first time, millions of people realized something powerful. Work did not have to look the way it always had. Productivity did not require hovering supervisors. Success did not demand exhaustion. People learned they could earn a paycheck from home without someone standing over their shoulder, draining their energy and adding unnecessary stress.

Even after COVID restrictions lifted, many companies never returned to the old model. Remote work stayed. Hybrid schedules stayed. Digital collaboration became normal. The idea that you must sacrifice peace to earn money began to dissolve. We entered an era where comfort, flexibility, and income could coexist, and once that door opened, it never fully closed again.

At the same time, digital products exploded. People began buying books online, learning online, journaling online, building businesses online, and consuming content from creators instead of corporations. Digital products became one of the greatest blessings of this era because they do something traditional businesses rarely could. They separate your earning power from your physical labor. One product created once can pay you again and again without demanding more of your time, more of your energy, or more of your presence.

This is wealth creation in the modern world. This is entrepreneurship without exhaustion. This is abundance without burnout. And it is available to you right now.

When I look back over my life, I think about all the seasons I worked so hard I barely had time to breathe. Running a salon for over two decades, raising four children, building a brand, trying to grow while simultaneously trying to heal, exhaustion was my normal. I believed that working hard was the price of success. I believed rest was something you earned later, if ever.

But once I discovered the digital world, I realized something powerful. There are entire streams of income waiting to bless you the moment you allow yourself to think bigger than labor.

When I wrote my first book, that was a digital seed. When I started designing journals, that was a digital seed. Puzzle books, affirmation books, eBooks, each one became an income stream that did not require me to stand behind a chair for ten hours, wake up at five in the morning, or push myself past my emotional capacity. Digital products allowed me to earn from my creativity, my experiences, my wisdom, and my voice, and they will do the same for you.

Every digital product you create becomes a silent employee. It works while you sleep. It works on holidays. It works during naps. It works while you are spending time with your family. It works when life knocks you down and you need to pause. That is the beauty of digital leverage. Your work continues even when you need rest.

To fully step into this revolution, you must release an outdated belief system that tells you money only comes through hard labor. That belief kept our parents and grandparents in survival mode, but it cannot accompany you into your future. This is a new era. This is a new mindset. This is a new opportunity. And digital products are the doorway.

You may not realize it yet, but you are already carrying digital product ideas inside of you. Your stories matter. Your expertise matters. Your life lessons matter. Your creative imagination matters. Your solutions to problems other people struggle with matter. All of it can be transformed into something someone will purchase, learn from, enjoy, or find comfort in.

If you have overcome something, you can teach it. If you have learned something, you can package it. If you have created something, you can sell it. If you love something, you can share it. If you survived something, you can guide others through it. Digital products turn your life into legacy and your knowledge into currency.

The reason this matters so much is because digital creation removes the ceiling. One book can reach thousands. One journal can help tens of thousands. One online product can impact people you may never meet in person. The scale is limitless. The more you learn, the more you create. The more you create, the more you earn. You become a brand. You become a teacher. You become a visionary. You become a creator of wealth on your own terms.

When God gives you a gift, He never intends for it to sit unused. Your creativity is not accidental. Your voice is not random. Your experiences were not wasted. Everything you lived through, everything you learned, everything you survived can become part of your prosperity.

The digital revolution is not only about money. It is about freedom. Freedom from rigid schedules. Freedom from physical limitations. Freedom from financial fear. Freedom from depending on a single income stream that keeps you stressed and overworked. It is the opportunity to build something once and allow it to bless you for years to come.

Digital products do not require perfection. They require presence. They require the courage to begin. They require a willingness to learn. They require the belief that your story, your voice, your talents, and your mind are worthy of being seen and compensated. And once you step into this space, something shifts inside you. Your confidence expands. Your creativity unlocks. Your vision becomes clearer.

You begin to understand that you were never created to merely survive. You were created to build, to multiply, to prosper, to impact, to rise. This is the digital age. This is the opportunity of your lifetime. This is the moment you choose creation over fear. This is the moment you choose abundance over exhaustion. This is the moment you step into your next level.

Your wealth is waiting. Your audience is waiting. Your breakthrough is waiting. And your digital products are the bridge that will take you there.

There is no denying that COVID was devastating. Lives were lost. Families were changed forever. Jobs disappeared. Fear entered homes across the world. For many people, it was the most painful season they have ever lived through. We grieved together, even while isolated. We learned how fragile life really is, and how quickly everything we depend on can change. Nothing about that time should be minimized or romanticized. It was real loss. Real fear. Real heartbreak.

And yet, even in the midst of catastrophe, something unexpected happened. The world slowed down. People were forced to come home. Commutes vanished. Time returned. For the first time, millions of people were no longer spending hours of their lives stuck in traffic or sitting under fluorescent lights being watched while they worked. The home became the center of life again. Families ate together. Parents saw their children grow. And people began to realize that productivity did not require suffering.

That shift opened a door that many people are still walking through today. Working from home became normal. Acceptable. Even preferred. And quietly, something else became possible. While still showing up for nine-to-five responsibilities, people were able to explore the ideas they had been postponing for years. The book they never had time to write. The business idea they kept pushing aside. The creative project that lived in their spirit but never fit into a rigid schedule. For the first time, dreams could coexist with a paycheck.

This is where the call to action lives. That window did not open by accident. It opened to show you what is possible when time, access, and courage meet. If you used that season to survive, honor yourself. If you used it to reflect, honor yourself. But if you feel a quiet pull to build something of your own now, do not ignore it. Tragedy shook the world, but it also revealed new pathways. The question is no longer whether it can be done from home. The question is whether you are willing to use what you learned to create a future that honors both your peace and your potential.

3

Side Hustle

For most people, a side hustle is born out of necessity. It begins as extra income, a little cushion, a little relief, a way to breathe when life feels tight. But what many don't realize is that side hustles are not small ideas. They are divine introductions. They are whispers from God saying, *"There is more for you than this. There is another door. Try it. Build it. Trust it."* Every empire begins with one small decision to try.

I never set out to run one of the most successful braiding salons in Los Angeles. I didn't know I would employ over 1,700 women or that my H2 Hummer would become the headquarters of my guerrilla marketing team. All I knew in the beginning was that I had a skill, a passion, and a desire to feed my children. That desire, that hunger, became my side hustle. And that side hustle grew into a full-time empire because I treated it like it mattered long before anyone else did.

This is the truth many people miss: your side hustle is not just extra money, it is a preview of your freedom. It is your training ground. It is your laboratory. It is where you practice, experiment, fail forward, and rise into the person you must become to live the life you truly desire. A side hustle is not small. It is seed. And seeds don't reveal their greatness in the beginning, they reveal it in the harvest.

Too many people underestimate the power of what they can build on the side. They think small because the vision is still small, but freedom requires you to think past your current circumstances. Freedom asks you to rise into your future self now, before the evidence appears. Every business that changed someone's life started in someone's living room, kitchen table, back bedroom, garage, or notebook. God does not wait for perfection. He waits for obedience. He waits for willingness. He waits for movement.

Full-time freedom is not one giant leap, it is a series of consistent, disciplined, faith-filled steps. It is showing up for your dream even when life pulls at you, even when you're tired, even when you're scared, even when no one else sees what you see. Freedom comes to those who refuse to quit.

The moment your side hustle becomes a priority, your life changes. When you begin carving out time for it instead of squeezing it into the leftover hours of your day, the universe takes notice. When you begin investing energy, improving your craft, studying your industry, expanding your creativity, and showing up with excellence, even while it's still small, something supernatural begins to shift. Doors open. Ideas flow. People notice. Favor increases. Because what you honor, expands.

I remember juggling motherhood, employees, client drama, marketing, payroll, life trauma, and still pushing forward because I believed in the vision God placed in me. I didn't wait for life to get easier, I built while life was hard. That is the difference between people who dream and people who rise. One waits for the perfect moment. The other creates momentum.

Your side hustle becomes a full-time life when you treat it as sacred. When you respect it. When you nurture it. When you allow it to stretch you. When you stop disqualifying yourself. When you stop calling it "little." When you stop letting fear speak louder than your assignment. Side hustles fail not because people lack talent, but because they lack belief. They quit too soon. They shrink too quickly. They assume slow results mean no results. But slow results are the beginning of stability. Every business needs time to root before it rises.

Freedom does not come from wishing. It comes from building. It comes from choosing. It comes from aligning your actions with your future, not your circumstances. One day, your side hustle will ask you a question: "Are you ready to trust me?" That moment will arrive when the income starts growing, when the opportunities increase, when your confidence expands, when the dream inside you becomes too large to fit into the leftover hours of your life. That is when you step into full-time freedom.

But here is the truth, freedom is not just financial. Freedom is emotional. Freedom is spiritual. Freedom is waking up without dread. Freedom is being present with your children. Freedom is creating on your own terms. Freedom is healing while earning. Freedom is becoming who you were always meant to be.

Your side hustle is the pathway to that kind of life. You don't have to quit your job today. You don't have to leap before you're ready. Just build intentionally. Build consistently. Build boldly. Build with faith. Build with discipline. Build with expectation that this small beginning is on its way to becoming something extraordinary.

Your dream is not accidental. Your talent is not accidental.

Your ideas are not accidental. God is not teasing you. He is preparing you. He is positioning you. And He is waiting for you to take the next step so He can bless the work of your hands.

One day, you will look back at this chapter of your life, the late nights, the early mornings, the moments of doubt, the small wins, the setbacks, the breakthroughs, and you will realize something powerful: your side hustle wasn't just building a business.

It was building *you*.

It was shaping your resilience.

It was strengthening your faith.

It was expanding your mind.

It was increasing your capacity.

It was preparing you for the life you prayed for.

Full-time freedom is not a fantasy. It is not reserved for the lucky. It is the result of intention, courage, consistency, creativity, and belief. If you can build it on the side, you can build it for life. If you can manage it in small form, you can manage it in abundance. And if you can believe in it before it pays you, you are already halfway free.

You are standing at the doorway of a new chapter. The question is not "Can I really do this?" The question is "Will I honor the gift God placed inside me?" Because when you do, your side hustle becomes your calling, and your calling becomes your freedom.

4

Financial Strategy

Most people assume wealth begins in a bank account, but you and I both know it starts long before that. It begins in the mind. Long before money ever shows up in your hands, it shows up in your thoughts, your expectations, and your sense of what you believe is possible for your life. If your thoughts are rooted in fear, lack, limitation, or "just enough," then even when money arrives, it often slips right through your fingers. You cannot build a wealthy life on a poverty mindset. It simply will not hold. Wealth requires a different internal foundation. You have to think differently, believe differently, and expect differently. I had to learn that firsthand.

Although I cannot say that I was consciously creating abundance in my mind at the very beginning of my journey, I now recognize that once I accepted the belief that everything starts internally, I always began there first. I did not understand it as a formal practice back then, but looking back, I can see that my mind was always laying the groundwork before my life caught up. The belief always came first, even when I was unaware of it.

Whatever business you are planning to make the source of your additional income, you must visualize that business first. Before you build it with your hands, you must build it with your mind. Before it becomes real in the world, it must become familiar in your imagination. If you cannot see yourself succeeding in it internally, you will unconsciously resist it externally.

Creative visualization has proven to be one of the most powerful tools in my life, which is why I want to share it with you in greater depth here. I briefly touched on this concept in earlier chapters, but it deserves more space because it changes everything. We have the power to close our eyes and imagine the things we desire as if they already exist. Pretending they exist is often the very doorway through which they enter our lives.

Children use their imagination effortlessly. They play, they pretend, they create entire worlds without hesitation. We are born with this natural ability to create vividly in our minds, but somewhere along the way, many of us were taught to abandon it. We were told to be realistic, to be practical, to lower our expectations. Yet holding thoughts and images in our minds until they feel real is one of the keys to bringing what we want into our lives. The thoughts we focus on are the ones that matter most. When we learn to guide them instead of letting them run wild, we begin to guide our lives.

Several books were instrumental in helping me understand the importance of stillness and mental awareness. Russell Simmons' *Super Rich* and *Success Through Stillness*, along with Eckhart Tolle's *The Power of Now*, helped shape how I view wealth and peace. *Super Rich* left a particularly deep impression on me. Many people are drawn to that title expecting secrets to financial success, but what Russell spoke about was spiritual and emotional wealth. He understood, as I later came to understand myself, that all the money in the world cannot give you peace of mind if your inner world is chaotic.

I get genuinely excited about the concepts I share in my books, and I have unshakable faith in them. Still, there have been many moments in my life when I had to actively apply every tool I believe in to recenter myself. Life has a way of delivering unexpected blows. During those moments, I had to pause, reevaluate, and reaffirm what I knew to be true instead of abandoning it under pressure. Starting a new business can indeed bring on pressure. My suggestion it to stop and take a breath when you feel yourself becoming overwhelmed. I remember noticing I was holding tension in my head and chest when I was in the middle of learning my new skill set for my new business. I would tense up and end up with a huge headache. I had to conscious start telling myself to release and breath. I would instantly notice the shift in my body and relax and continue. I understand why I was doing it. there is so much riding on you not failing. That tension represent not just determination but fear. You must release the fear so you don't end up aging ten years by the opening of the business.

In the early days of business, there was a time in my life when I hustled purely out of survival. I was not thinking about millions, passive income, or generational wealth. I was thinking about keeping the lights on, feeding my children, and paying off my mortgage. Growing up around addiction, instability, and emotional abandonment trained my nervous system to expect struggle. It taught me that suffering was normal and that life would always feel like running from one crisis to the next. I lived that way for a long time. My business was a success, but it definitely was not void of stress. I knew that I wanted the second half of my life, the season where I made money from home, to be easy, fun, and peaceful.

When your nervous system is trained for survival, you do not naturally plan for overflow. You plan for emergencies. You dream safely instead of boldly. You brace for impact instead of building for expansion. That is the quiet damage of a poverty mindset. It does not just affect money. It affects how you imagine your future, how far you allow yourself to dream, and how much ease you believe you are allowed to experience.

What I eventually realized was that my body and my mind were still operating as if danger was always around the corner, even when stability was already present. I had learned how to build, how to hustle, and how to endure, but I had not yet learned how to rest inside success. That shift did not happen overnight. It required intention. It required retraining my thoughts, my expectations, and my relationship with money so that peace could finally coexist with prosperity.

That is why making money in this next season had to look different for me. It could no longer be rooted in stress, urgency, or exhaustion. It had to be rooted in alignment, sustainability, and joy. I did not want to just earn more. I wanted to live better. And once I gave myself permission to want that, everything about how I approached wealth began to change.

At some point, something inside me shifted. It was subtle but undeniable. A whisper. A thought. A knowing. There has to be more than this. That moment was not about money. It was about worth. It was about finally questioning the belief that struggle was my permanent state.

That is where wealth truly begins. It begins the moment your spirit says, "I am worthy of more." Not because your circumstances suddenly change, but because you stop treating yourself as if you are undeserving. Your income will only rise to the level of what you believe you are allowed to have. If deep down you believe you are unworthy, you will sabotage opportunities without even realizing it.

When I first started Braids By SaBrina, I was not thinking like a business owner. I was thinking like a survivor. I was doing hair because I had to. But necessity has a way of introducing you to your calling. Over time, the hustle became strategy. The struggle became skill. Survival turned into leadership. That small business I started from my home became the foundation of a mindset that carried me through decades of entrepreneurship.

Sometimes your first hustle is not your final destination. Sometimes it is your training ground. It is proof that you can be consistent, that you can learn, that you can lead, and that you can finish what you start.

Mindset is the real millionaire seed. Money follows belief. Opportunity follows expectation. Breakthrough follows identity. These are not slogans. They are laws of life. The way you see yourself determines what you attempt. The way you speak to yourself determines how far you go.

As you step into your future, you must release the beliefs that poverty taught you. The world has changed. Access has changed. Technology has changed. The earning potential inside your home has changed. But if your thinking does not change, none of that matters.

Expanding your mindset expands your income because it changes how you move. You stop waiting to be chosen and you choose yourself. You stop asking for permission and you give it to yourself.

Wealth today is created through intention, discipline, creativity, and the willingness to learn. You do not need a perfect background. You do not need to know everything. You need a decision.

Wealth is not only money. Wealth is peace. Wealth is options. Wealth is rest. Wealth is being able to say no without fear. When your mind aligns with abundance, your actions follow.

I have owned businesses I knew nothing about before opening them. Inked 4 Life Tattoo Studio began as a thought. I had no experience in the tattoo industry. Yet I designed that business in my mind before it ever existed in reality. I visualized it. I acted on it. And within thirty days, it was real.

Our minds are extraordinary. Even before I understood visualization as a formal tool, I was using it instinctively. Fear and doubt did not get invited into the process. That is why it worked.

We are creators. Anything we truly desire is possible when we train our minds to believe it. This should be taught early in life. Children should be taught that they hold the crayons to their own lives.

Your wealth begins with a declaration. You are worthy of money. You are capable of earning more. You are open to overflow. You deserve financial peace. Repeating this rewires belief.

Those who thrive will be those who think bigger, adapt faster, and believe without hesitation. This book is not just about making money. It is about removing the internal blocks that stop it from flowing.

Money is energy. It reflects identity. When you shift from "I am just trying to make it" to "I am a creator of wealth," the world responds differently, and suddenly, you are not chasing money anymore. Money begins finding you. Not because of luck, but because you finally aligned with who you were always meant to be.

Making more money is not about chasing every opportunity. It is about becoming the kind of person opportunities recognize. Money moves toward clarity, confidence, and consistency. When you stop seeing yourself as someone hoping for a break and start seeing yourself as someone building a system, everything changes. You no longer ask, "Will this work for me?" You ask, "How will I make this work?" That shift alone separates dreamers from earners.

One of the biggest reasons people struggle financially is not a lack of ability, but a lack of self-trust. They second-guess their ideas. They abandon plans halfway through. They talk themselves out of action before momentum has a chance to build. You must become someone who honors their own ideas long enough to see results. Wealth rewards follow-through. It responds to people who show up even when motivation fades and doubt tries to take the wheel.

You also have to understand that discomfort is part of expansion. Learning new skills, navigating technology, putting yourself out there, and charging for your value can feel uncomfortable at first. That does not mean you are doing something wrong. It means you are growing. Comfort keeps you familiar. Discomfort moves you forward. Every financially secure person you admire once stood exactly where you are now, uncertain but willing to try anyway.

Making more money also requires releasing old loyalty to struggle. Some people subconsciously hold onto financial hardship because it feels familiar or because they associate ease with guilt. You must give yourself permission to succeed without apology. You are not betraying your past by doing better. You are honoring it by refusing to stay stuck in survival mode. Prosperity does not make you selfish. It makes you stable, generous, and free.

Finally, remember this. Money is not the goal. Freedom is. Security and Peace of mind is. Choice is. The ability to breathe without financial pressure is life-changing. When you commit to making more money, you are not just changing your income. You are changing your nervous system. You are changing how you show up for your family. You are changing what you believe is possible for your future. And once that belief locks in, nothing can stop what you are building.

5

Make Money While You Sleep

There comes a moment in every person's life when they realize working harder is not the same as earning more. Hustle has its place, but hustle cannot be your whole life. The body gets tired. The mind gets overwhelmed. Children grow older. Seasons change. Life asks more of you than clocking in and clocking out ever could.

That's when you understand why true wealth isn't built from the hours you work, it's built from the **systems you build**, the **assets you create**, and the **streams that continue to flow even when you're not awake to oversee them.**

This is income that breathes on its own.

Income that does not depend on your physical presence.

Income that honors your time instead of draining it.

Income that works while you sleep.

You deserve that.

Most of us grew up watching our parents work themselves into exhaustion. We were taught that hard labor equals success, that long hours equal loyalty, that fatigue equals achievement. But that mindset belonged to a generation that did not have the access we have today.

They didn't have online platforms.

They didn't have digital products.

They didn't have automated systems.

They didn't have global reach from their living room.

We do.

And refusing to take advantage of it is like refusing a blessing God already placed in your hands.

When I look back over my own life, I realize how many years I traded hours for dollars without understanding the spiritual law of multiplication. God never intended for you to survive off one source. In nature, everything reproduces. Everything expands. Everything contains the ability to become more.

So do you.

Residual income is simply financial reproduction, money multiplying from the seeds you've already planted. Think of it as the harvest from yesterday's work feeding tomorrow's life.

And this type of income requires one thing:

A mental shift from labor to leverage.

You must start asking yourself:

"What can I create one time that pays me repeatedly?"

"What knowledge do I carry that can be packaged?"

"What solution have I figured out that others desperately need?"

"What can I build this month that continues to bless me next year?"

Because wealthy people know something most people never learn:

The goal is not to work until you die.
The goal is to build something that works for you.

When you begin creating income that works while you sleep, you step into a new identity, the identity of someone who earns through wisdom, not weariness...through systems, not stress.

This shift is spiritual as much as it is financial.

Residual income honors your value.

It honors your time.

It honors your gifts.

It honors the God in you.

There is nothing holy about struggle.

There is nothing noble about burnout.

There is nothing admirable about carrying the entire weight of your life alone.

Abundance is not disobedience, it is alignment.

The moment you understand that, you stop limiting yourself to one paycheck, one opportunity, or one lane. You start realizing how much you already have to offer the world.

Think about this:

You have experience someone would pay to learn.

You have a story someone needs to hear.

You have a skill someone is desperately searching for.

You have knowledge someone wishes they had.

Every one of those things can become passive or residual income if you structure them correctly.

This chapter is not about convincing you to chase money. It's about waking up the part of you that knows you were created for more than exhaustion. You were created for overflow. You were designed for expansion. You were equipped for prosperity long before you ever learned the language of limitation.

The fear you feel around creating passive income isn't fear, it's unfamiliarity. You've simply never seen yourself outside of survival mode. But the truth is, the moment you activate your creativity and discipline, you become unstoppable.

Residual income is not built overnight, but it is built **for** your nights. It shows up while you rest. It grows while you heal. It circulates while you recharge. It becomes the silent partner in your success story.

And the best part?

Once you create one stream of income that works while you sleep, your mind automatically begins looking for the next one. Once your soul tastes ease, it refuses to return to struggle.

You were not born to live paycheck to paycheck.

You were not born to spend your life exhausted.

You were not born to fear the future.

You were born to create.

To expand.

To multiply.

To receive.

To thrive.

The people who win are not the ones who work the hardest — they are the ones who work the smartest, the most intentionally, and the most spiritually aligned.

You deserve income that honors your value even when your eyes are closed.

Now let's start building it.

6

Use Your Skills

When people hear the phrase *"multiple streams of income,"* they often imagine something complicated, overwhelming, or reserved for people with degrees, connections, or perfect lives. But let me tell you the truth, most of the wealthiest people you'll ever meet didn't get rich from one job or one opportunity. They got rich because they learned how to turn what they already had into something more, and that is exactly what you are going to learn to do. You don't need to start with millions. You don't need a fancy building. You don't need investors. **You start with your skills.**

When I built my businesses, it wasn't because someone handed me a blueprint. It was because I recognized that my hands, my gift, could save me. What I didn't realize at the time was that I was laying the foundation for multiple income streams long before I ever knew what that phrase meant.

I monetized what I knew. I packaged what I was good at. I charged for my time, my talent, and my technique. That is a stream, and here is the part most people miss. A skill becomes a stream the moment you decide it is worth money.

For years, I gave my books away for free because I did not want the price of a book to keep anyone from receiving the message. Initially, I wrote for healing, and that truly worked. I grew mentally, emotionally, and spiritually through becoming an author and sharing my story. That season had its purpose, and I do not regret a single book I ever gave away. I always knew there would come a day when I would launch a major advertising campaign for all of my books and begin selling them intentionally, finally creating residual income from the work I had already done.

My books served one important purpose first, to assist me with healing past trauma. Then they served a second purpose, to bring additional income into my life. Both purposes mattered. One did not cancel out the other. Healing and prosperity are allowed to coexist.

People spend their whole lives overlooking the very talent that could set them free. They say, "Oh, it's just something I do," without realizing that nothing is "just something" when God put purpose behind it. What comes naturally to you often holds the greatest value, not because it is easy for others, but because it is aligned for you.

If you can write, teach, cook, braid, design, organize, motivate, fix things, make people laugh, or make people feel seen, you already have streams inside you. You are not lacking ideas. You are lacking activation. The moment you stop minimizing what you carry and start treating it with respect, it begins to produce.

What most people do not understand is that income does not only come from doing more. It comes from doing what you already know how to do in a smarter, more intentional way. You do not need to reinvent yourself. You need to recognize your value, package it properly, and allow it to work for you beyond the hours you can physically show up.

This is how streams are built. Not all at once, not overnight, but decision by decision. The decision to stop giving everything away. The decision to honor your gift. The decision to believe that your purpose is allowed to provide for you.

Activation begins with awareness. Monetization begins with confidence. There were times when I didn't know I was building wealth, I was simply using what I had. But every skill I sharpened became a future income stream waiting for its moment to shine.

Braiding turned into:

– A salon
– Training students
– Selling techniques
– Paid speaking engagements
– Business education
– Life coaching
– Branding
– Writing Books
– Publishing Books for others

That is the blueprint. **One skill. Many streams.**

What you have inside you can multiply the same way. But here's the real key: You must stop thinking of your gifts as casual. Your gifts are currency. Your creativity is currency. Your story is currency. Your expertise, even if informal, is currency. It's time to stop giving it away for free.

We live in a time where anything you know, anything you've survived, anything you've mastered, can be monetized. The internet made everything accessible. But accessibility means nothing if you don't see your own value.

The shift happens the moment you stop asking, "Can I?" and start saying, "I will."

Turning your skills into streams requires a few internal agreements:

1. You must believe your gift is worthy of payment.

Not appreciation. Not applause. **Payment.**

People pay for expertise every day. Why not yours?

2. You must stop shrinking your abilities down to what others expect.

Just because everyone around you thinks small doesn't mean you have to join them.

3. You must embrace being a beginner in new areas.

Every new stream will stretch you — in the best way.

4. You must stop waiting for the world to crown you.

Name your price and stand behind it.

When I was younger, every single income stream I created was fueled by hunger, not desperation, but hunger to change my life, my family, my legacy. I believed that if I worked my gift, my gift would work for me. And it did.

Today, you have even more opportunity than I did. You can turn anything into a stream if your mindset is aligned:

– Do you love helping people? That's a stream.

– Do people always ask you for advice? That's a stream.

– Do you have a passion others don't? That's a stream.
– Do you know how to solve a problem? That's a stream.

The question is not **"Do you have a skill?"** The question is **"Are you ready to turn your skill into income?"** Because this is not the year for playing small.

It is not the year for hiding your gifts.

It is not the year for sitting on potential.

It is the year of **expansion.**

It is the year of **activation.**

It is the year of **multiple streams.**

And the beautiful thing about turning skills into streams is this:

Truth is, I did not have multiple streams of income for thirty years. Everything I made came from my salon. I worked a lot in my own chair, and I always had braiders who worked for me and paid me 40%, but every dime still came out of that one business. I was blessed, and I'm grateful for what that salon provided for me and my family, but imagine if something had happened to the salon and I was forced to close. I had nothing else. That worked for me during a different time, a different economy, and a different season of life. I would not advise anyone to do that in today's market.

Because the truth is, depending on one stream is like balancing your whole life on one leg. It can stand, and it can hold you for a while, but all it takes is one unexpected shift and suddenly you're wobbling. One medical scare. One slow season. One major life change. One economic downturn. One new competitor. One policy change. One thing you didn't plan for, and now your stability is in question. It doesn't mean you failed. It means the world is unpredictable, and wisdom prepares for unpredictability.

Back then, I didn't think like that. I thought, "As long as the doors are open, I'm good." I thought, "As long as my hands can work, money will come." And for years, it did. The salon was my identity, my security, my plan, and my proof that I could make it. But the problem with putting everything into one basket is not that the basket is bad, it's that life can shake the basket. And when you have multiple streams, life can shake one stream without shaking your whole world.

That is why, building multiple streams of income isn't just a money move, it's a peace move. It's emotional security. It's mental stability. It's being able to breathe. It's being able to make decisions from power instead of panic. It's not having to stay in something that's draining you because you're afraid of losing your only source of income. Multiple streams give you options, and options are a form of freedom.

And I need you to hear this clearly: you do not have to be famous, rich, or "techy" to build more than one stream. You just have to be intentional. You already have skills. You already have experience. You already have knowledge someone else needs. And when you learn how to package that knowledge, offer that service, or create that product in more than one way, you are no longer limited to one paycheck, one location, or one lane. You stop surviving on one stream, and you start building a financial foundation that can hold you up—no matter what changes.

So if you are reading this and you currently have one stream, don't feel ashamed. Feel informed. Feel awakened. Let this be your confirmation that it's time to expand. Keep your main thing, but build around it. Protect yourself. Protect your future.

Protect your peace. Because the goal isn't just to make money, it's to make sure your life is never one unexpected event away from financial fear again.

You do not have to do everything at once. You just have to begin.

Start with one skill, the strongest one, the one people compliment you on, the one you enjoy enough to stick with. Give that skill structure, pricing, packaging, and purpose. Once that stream is flowing, another will rise. And another. And another.

Because once a person learns how to monetize themselves, they never go back to depending on one income source again.

You are gifted. You are capable. You are already equipped. Now let's turn your skills into streams that bless your household for years to come.

7

Residual Income

There has never been a time in history where ordinary people had this much access, this much opportunity, and this much creative freedom. For generations, wealth was locked behind gates of education, privilege, location, and positions most of us were never invited into. You had to know the right people, be in the right place, or wait for someone to open a door for you. But the digital world changed everything. It leveled the playing field. It removed the gate and quietly handed the keys to anyone willing to learn, create, and show up.

Today, you do not need permission to prosper. You do not need approval to create. You do not need credentials to publish. You do not need investors to get started. What you need now is clarity, consistency, and the courage to finally transform your gifts into income. This era rewards people who are willing to stop waiting and start building.

Then COVID happened, and the world shifted in a way no one could have predicted. Offices shut down. Commutes disappeared overnight. Dining room tables became desks. Living rooms became studios. Kitchens became classrooms. And for the first time, millions of people realized something powerful. Work did not have to look the way it always had. Productivity did not require hovering supervisors. Success did not demand exhaustion. People learned they could earn a paycheck from home without someone standing over their shoulder, draining their energy and adding unnecessary stress.

Even after COVID restrictions lifted, many companies never returned to the old model. Remote work stayed. Hybrid sched-ules stayed. Digital collaboration became normal. The idea that you must sacrifice peace to earn money began to dissolve. We entered an era where comfort, flexibility, and income could coexist, and once that door opened, it never fully closed again.

At the same time, digital products exploded. People began buy-ing books online, learning online, journaling online, building businesses online, and consuming content from creators instead of corporations. Digital products became one of the greatest blessings of this era because they do something traditional businesses rarely could. They separate your earning power from your physical labor. One product created once can pay you again and again without demanding more of your time, more of your energy, or more of your presence.

This is wealth creation in the modern world. This is en-trepreneurship without exhaustion. This is abundance without burnout. And it is available to you right now.

When I look back over my life, I think about all the seasons I worked so hard I barely had time to breathe. Running a salon for over two decades, raising four children, building a brand, trying to grow while simultaneously trying to heal, exhaustion was my normal. I believed that working hard was the price of success. I believed rest was something you earned later, if ever. But once I discovered the digital world, I realized something powerful. There are entire streams of income waiting to bless you the moment you allow yourself to think bigger than labor.

When I wrote my first book, that was a digital seed. When I started designing journals, that was a digital seed. Puzzle books, affirmation books, eBooks, each one became an income stream that did not require me to stand behind a chair for ten hours, wake up at five in the morning, or push myself past my emotional capacity. Digital products allowed me to earn from my creativity, my experiences, my wisdom, and my voice, and they will do the same for you.

Every digital product you create becomes a silent employee. It works while you sleep. It works on holidays. It works during naps. It works while you are spending time with your family. It works when life knocks you down and you need to pause. That is the beauty of digital leverage. Your work continues even when you need rest.

To fully step into this revolution, you must release an outdated belief system that tells you money only comes through hard labor. This is a new era. This is a new mindset. This is a new opportunity. And digital products are the doorway.

You may not realize it yet, but you are already carrying digital product ideas inside of you. Your stories matter. Expertise matters. Life lessons matter. Your creative imagination matters. Your solutions to problems other people struggle with matter. All of it can be transformed into something someone will purchase, learn from, enjoy, or find comfort in.

If you have overcome something, you can teach it. If you have learned something, you can package it. If you have created something, you can sell it. If you love something, you can share it. If you survived something, you can guide others through it. Digital products turn your life into legacy and your knowledge into currency.

The reason this matters so much is because digital creation removes the ceiling. One book can reach thousands. One journal can help tens of thousands. One online product can impact people you may never meet in person. The scale is limitless. The more you learn, the more you create. The more you create, the more you earn. You become a brand. You become a teacher. You become a visionary. You become a creator of wealth on your own terms.

When God gives you a gift, He never intends for it to sit unused. Your creativity is not accidental. Your voice is not random. Your experiences were not wasted. Everything you lived through, everything you learned, everything you survived can become part of your prosperity.

The digital revolution is not only about money. It is about freedom. Freedom from rigid schedules. Freedom from physical limitations. Freedom from financial fear. Freedom from depending on a single income stream that keeps you stressed and overworked. It is the opportunity to build something once and allow it to bless you for years to come.

Digital products do not require perfection. They require presence. They require the courage to begin. They require a willingness to learn. They require the belief that your story, your voice, your talents, and your mind are worthy of being seen and compensated. And once you step into this space, something shifts inside you. Your confidence expands. Your creativity unlocks. Your vision becomes clearer.

You begin to understand that you were never created to merely survive. You were created to build, to multiply, to prosper, to impact, to rise. This is the digital age. This is the opportunity of your lifetime. This is the moment you choose creation over fear. This is the moment you choose abundance over exhaustion. This is the moment you step into your next level.

Your wealth is waiting. Your audience is waiting. Your breakthrough is waiting. And your digital products are the bridge that will take you there.

There is no denying that COVID was devastating. Lives were lost. Families were changed forever. Jobs disappeared. Fear entered homes across the world. For many people, it was the most painful season they have ever lived through. We grieved together, even while isolated. We learned how fragile life really is, and how quickly everything we depend on can change. Nothing about that time should be minimized or romanticized. It was real loss. Real fear. Real heartbreak.

And yet, even in the midst of catastrophe, something unexpected happened. The world slowed down. People were forced to come home. Commutes vanished. Time returned. For the first time, millions of people were no longer spending hours of their lives stuck in traffic or sitting under fluorescent lights being watched while they worked. The home became the center of life again. Families ate together. Parents saw their children grow. And people began to realize that productivity did not require suffering.

That shift opened a door that many people are still walking through today. Working from home became normal. Acceptable. Even preferred. And quietly, something else became possible. While still showing up for nine-to-five responsibilities, people were able to explore the ideas they had been postponing for years. The book they never had time to write. The business idea they kept pushing aside. The creative project that lived in their spirit but never fit into a rigid schedule. For the first time, dreams could coexist with a paycheck.

This is where the call to action lives. That window did not open by accident. It opened to show you what is possible when time, access, and courage meet. If you used that season to survive, honor yourself. If you used it to reflect, honor yourself. But if you feel a quiet pull to build something of your own now, do not ignore it. Tragedy shook the world, but it also revealed new pathways. The question is no longer whether it can be done from home. The question is whether you are willing to use what you learned to create a future that honors both your peace and your potential.

One of the most powerful shifts you can make in this season of your life is moving from the idea of "one job" to the idea of "multiple streams." Not because you are greedy, but because you are wise. One income stream keeps you dependent. Multiple income streams give you options. They give you breathing room. They give you peace. Residual income, in particular, allows your past effort to support your present and future life.

Residual income does not mean effortless income. It means intentional income. It means you build something once, nurture it, and allow it to continue working even when you are not physically present. It is the difference between trading hours for dollars and building assets that serve you long after the initial work is done. That shift alone can change how safe you feel in your body and how hopeful you feel about your future.

Many people already have ideas for residual income, but they dismiss them before they ever give them a chance. They say things like, "That's already been done," or "Who would buy that from me?" or "I don't know enough yet." But every successful income stream started as a thought someone almost ignored. Ideas do not come to everyone. They come to people who are meant to act on them.

This is why it is so important to slow down and actually listen to what has been mulling through your mind. Pay attention to the ideas that keep returning. The ones that show up when you are driving. The ones that surface when you are tired. The ones that feel exciting and intimidating at the same time. Those are not random thoughts. Those are invitations.

Residual income streams often come from three places: what you know, what you love, and what you have lived through. Sometimes it is a skill you use every day. Sometimes it is a problem you solved for yourself. Sometimes it is a passion you have never given yourself permission to monetize. The key is not perfection. The key is exploration.

Once you begin identifying possible income streams, your next responsibility is research. Research turns ideas into plans. It removes fear by replacing it with information. It helps you see what is working, what is over-saturated, and where you might fit naturally. Research is not about copying someone else's path. It is about understanding the landscape so you can choose your own direction wisely.

Research also protects you from wasting time and energy. Instead of jumping into something blindly, you begin to ask better questions. Who is this for? What problem does it solve? How are people already buying this type of product or service? What would make mine different? These questions sharpen your thinking and strengthen your confidence.

As you research each idea, you may notice that some excite you more than others. Pay attention to that. Residual income works best when it aligns with who you are, not who you think you should be. You are building something that may be with you for years. Choose ideas you can grow with, not ones that drain you before they ever pay you.

Do not rush this process. Give yourself permission to brain-storm without judgment. Some ideas will evolve. Some will fall away. Some will surprise you. The goal of this exercise is not to decide everything today. The goal is to open the door to possibility and begin thinking like someone who builds income intentionally.

Before moving forward, take a moment to write down your ideas. These are not commitments yet. They are starting points. Let them be honest. Let them be imperfect. Let them be yours.

Write down six to eight possible residual income ideas below:

1.
2.
3.
4.
5.
6.
7.
8.

Now, choose **one idea at a time** and begin researching it. Do not try to do all of them at once. Focus creates clarity.

Here are a few simple places to start your research for each idea:

- **YouTube:** Search for creators already working in that niche. Watch how they explain what they do, what products they offer, and who their audience is. Pay attention to comments and questions people are asking. See what people love and what they feel is missing.

- **Google:** Search basic questions about your idea and notice what keeps coming up. This shows demand and common challenges.
- **Social Media:** Observe how people talk about this topic. Look at what content gets engagement and what problems people are openly expressing.

As you research, write down what you learn. Notice patterns. Notice gaps. Notice where your voice, experience, or creativity could naturally fit. This is how an idea begins turning into an income stream.

Remember, you do not need to have everything figured out to begin. You only need to be willing to explore. Residual income is not built by waiting for certainty. It is built by taking small, informed steps forward.

This chapter is not asking you to change your life overnight. It is asking you to think differently about your future. You are capable of building income that supports you, even when you are resting. And the ideas you just wrote down may be the very streams that make that possible.

8

Monetizing Matters

Let me be real with you.

You do not need a new degree. You do not need permission. You do not need to wait. You already have enough experience, lessons, and life-earned wisdom to start making money right now. This chapter is not about theory. It is about taking what is already inside you, your knowledge, your scars, your skills, and turning them into income, impact, and independence. It is about finally understanding that what you carry has value, and that value deserves compensation.

There was a time when I did not fully understand that. I thought purpose meant giving everything away. I thought being spiritual meant being soft. I thought love meant access without boundaries. What I learned the hard way is that purpose does not cancel payment, and compassion does not require self-sacrifice to the point of depletion.

You have been sitting on a gold mine.

The things you have already survived, built, created, or figured out are not just memories. They are intellectual property. They are value. They are money.

The way I knew how to braid hair with no formal training was value.

The way I kept a shop full of stylists motivated even when I was broke and broken was leadership training.

The way I wrote fliers, opened barbershops, created tattoo studios, and built all of them from the ground up was a masterclass.

So what do you know how to do? What do people call you for?

What could you teach if someone handed you a microphone today?

That is your product. That is your program. That is your platform. Start There!

We live in a world where people are charging high prices for information they Googled last year. Some are selling weekend courses and mentorships without ever running a real business. So imagine what you are worth, someone who actually lived it, built it, survived it, and figured it out the hard way.

You do not need to fake it until you make it because you have already lived it until you began earning with it.

-If you have been through divorce and came out stronger, that wisdom has value.

-If you raised children while building a business, that blueprint has value.

-If you navigated loss, depression, betrayal, and still found God, that is coaching.

-If you built businesses before the internet even existed, that is rare knowledge.

You are not starting over. You are stacking on top of what you already built.

Now let me talk to you about something that stops a lot of people right here. Friends and family. This is where many people fold. They feel guilty charging the people they love. They feel awkward stating their price. They soften their boundaries and shrink their value because they do not want to seem greedy or mean.

Let me say this clearly. You must charge everybody. You are allowed to offer a discount if you choose, but you must charge everybody. If you do not learn how to say your price out loud, you will struggle in business. If you cannot look someone in the eye and calmly state your fee, your confidence will crack under pressure. This is not about being cold. This is about being clear. People respect clarity.

You are not responsible for anyone's comfort around your growth. You are responsible for honoring your time, your energy, and your expertise. You did not survive what you survived to work for free. You did not study, practice, build, fail, and rebuild to be guilted into giving it away.

If someone questions your price, that does not mean you lower it. It means they are not your client. Part of entrepreneurship is developing a backbone. A peaceful one, but a firm one. One that knows the market, understands the value, and stands confidently in the number you chose. Do the research. Look at what others are charging for similar services. Know your worth in context. Then stand on it.

Now let us talk about money management, because income without structure leads to stress. When starting a new business venture, you must decide ahead of time what you are willing to invest. This is how you protect yourself.

You do not take money away from vital needs. You do not gamble with rent, mortgage, car notes, or food. You build intentionally and responsibly.

Here is where you start with your budget:

-Decide the maximum amount you are willing to invest initially

-Identify extra or flexible income that is not tied to essentials

-Set aside money specifically for learning, tools, or promotion

-Commit to staying within that budget during the early phase

This discipline builds confidence. It keeps fear from running the show. It allows you to grow without panic.

Now let us return to monetizing what you know.You do not need an office. You need a phone. You do not need permission. You need consistency and unshakable resilience.

I built half my empire with a marker and neon poster board. Today, you have Instagram, YouTube, Canva, Zoom, and a global audience in your pocket. Use it.

Share your knowledge and post what you know. Talk about what you lived and teach others what you survived. Someone is praying for and willing to pay for the clarity you already have.

Stop feeling bad about charging. Stop shrinking your gifts. Stop acting like the answer God gave you is supposed to be free to everyone else while costing you everything.

You are not charging for time. You are charging for results. You are charging for healing. You are charging for the shortcut you had to earn through pain.

You are the brand and the proof is your life.

You are the curriculum so you do not need a full website initially.

You do not need to spent money on a manager. You do not need to overthink it.

Pick something you know and Lets Go!

Choose a simple way to share it. Put a price on it. You can always alter the price later but make a final decision and tell the world. Utilize the free promotion on social media.

If God gave you the survival skills, He will give you the strategy and you already have the content. The content is inside of you. Pull it out and let it work for you.

In today's market its all about Monetization. So monetize what you know and what you have lived through. Monetize what tried to break you but did not. Because someone needs what you already overcame, and they will gladly pay to learn from someone who kept it real.

Don't sit on your story. Do not tuck away your brilliance waiting for a perfect moment that may never come. You walked through storms others are still praying to survive. You built what others are still trying to understand. You turned pain into power, and now it is time to turn that power into profit.

You are not starting from scratch. You are starting from experience, and experience is the most valuable currency on Earth.

You are not chasing opportunity anymore. You are the opportunity!

9

Get Branded

Branding isn't just logos and colors. Branding is energy. It is the unspoken message people feel when they hear your name, see your face, or read your words. It is what people experience even when you are not in the room. Before anyone buys from you, hires you, or trusts you, they feel you. That feeling is your brand.

You do not brand a business before you brand yourself. Who are you? What do you stand for? What does your presence say before you even speak? You are your brand. Your story, your style, your walk, your words, your consistency, all of it is part of the message you are sending into the world every single day.

When I was building Braids By SaBrina, there was no Canva, no branding courses, no social media templates, and no step by step guide. My brand was me. I was a young Black woman in Compton with purpose in my hands and a vision in my spirit. I wore it. I spoke it. I passed out fliers that told people, this is who I am and this is what I do. Long before I understood branding as a concept, I was living it.

One of the most important branding decisions I ever made

was color. My salons, Braids By SaBrina and later A New Vision Dreadlock Studio, were purple. Everything was purple. The walls, the fliers, the business cards, the energy. People knew it. They recognized it. They expected it. Purple became synonymous with my work, my creativity, and my excellence.

Something beautiful happened because I stayed consistent. My clients started associating that purple with how they felt when they came to see me. Safe. Seen. Beautiful. Empowered. Some of them even began bringing me purple gifts when they went shopping. Purple vases. Purple décor. Little purple trinkets they thought I would like. That is what happens when branding moves beyond aesthetics and becomes emotional connection.

I never changed it. I never got bored with it. I did not chase trends. I trusted what worked. That consistency built familiarity, and familiarity built trust. Trust is what keeps people coming back. Trust is what turns clients into supporters and supporters into ambassadors.

That same principle carries into my books today. When you look at most of my covers, you will see Royal Blue, Navy Blue, Magenta, and White. Those are my brand colors. Occasionally, I will introduce one additional color to give myself creative flexibility, but the foundation always stays the same. People are used to seeing that magenta and that blue. It feels familiar to them. It feels like me.

Those colors were chosen intentionally. Men see the blue and do not feel like the message is only for women. Women see the magenta and do not feel like the message is only for men. The brand feels inclusive, balanced, and welcoming. Without a single word being spoken, the colors are already communicating who the message is for.

That is the power of intentional branding. It speaks before

you do. It sets the tone before someone opens the book. It tells people whether they belong before they ever read the first page.

The most successful brands are not always the loudest or the flashiest. They are the most consistent. Consistency builds trust, and trust creates opportunity. When people know what to expect from you, they feel safe investing in you, recommending you, and supporting your work.

Branding yourself is not about becoming who people expect. It is about becoming unforgettable by being exactly who you are. That means showing up with your truth, your values, your voice, even when it feels uncomfortable. Especially when it feels uncomfortable. Authenticity cannot be replicated, and people feel it immediately.

Your reputation will often open doors before your resume ever does. People will talk about how you made them feel. They will remember how you showed up. They will notice whether your words and actions align. That is branding in its purest form.

Think of yourself as a walking billboard. Every post, every conversation, every email, every service interaction is shaping the brand called you. Are you dependable? Are you passionate? Are you professional? Do you keep your word? Or do you cut corners and make excuses? Your brand is being built whether you are intentional about it or not. So you might as well build it on purpose.

When I built my brand, I did it in the streets, literally. I handed out thousands of fliers. I showed up consistently. I treated people with respect. I honored my word. Over time, that became the SaBrina Fisher Reece brand. Not just a salon. Not just a service. A standard.

That same opportunity exists for you. Branding is not reserved for celebrities or corporations. It belongs to anyone willing to decide who they are and show up as that person consistently. When your brand is clear, the right people find you without you chasing them. Doors open quietly. Invitations come unexpectedly. Opportunities appear without you forcing them.

When you align your brand with who you truly are, everything becomes easier. You stop pretending. You stop explaining. You stop shrinking. Your presence does the work for you. That is when your brand becomes an asset that works even when you are not trying.

Branding is not decoration. It is declaration. It is the statement you make to the world about who you are, what you value, and what people can expect when they engage with you. Build it with intention. Protect it with consistency. And let it carry you into rooms you never imagined entering.

That is the power of branding yourself for unlimited opportunities.

10

Constant Cash Flow

Let's talk about money, not just making it, but keeping it moving. Consistent cash flow is the difference between being in business and being in stress. It's the bloodline of your brand, and if it stops, everything stops. Most entrepreneurs don't fail because they aren't talented. They fail because their income is unpredictable. One month they're up, the next they're in panic mode, robbing Peter to pay Paul. But that's not the life we're building over here. We're building legacy, structure, and sustainability.

To master cash flow, you have to think beyond the hustle. The goal isn't to just make quick money, it's to build systems that keep the money coming even when you're tired, sick, or on vacation. I learned early on that my hands could only braid so many heads in a week. But my knowledge? My methods? My story? That could reach thousands. So I wrote books, launched classes, and created ways for money to find me while I slept. That's the power of passive income, money that doesn't depend on you showing up in person every time.

But even with systems in place, consistency requires discipline. You have to track every dollar. Watch your spending. Stop emotional swiping. Know your slow seasons before they hit and prepare for them. You can't pray for financial blessings and be careless with the ones you already have. I've seen so many entrepreneurs make thousands and still end up broke because they didn't respect the flow. Respecting money means knowing what's coming in, what's going out, and what's being wasted.

One of the best things I ever did for my cash flow was start saving with every transaction. Every client. Every sale. Every product. I trained myself to take a portion and tuck it away. Not after I paid bills, *before.* Because if you wait until it's left over, it never will be. You don't need to be rich to start saving. You just need to be consistent. That small habit creates a cushion, and that cushion keeps you from crumbling when life hits hard, because trust me, it will.

Here's the truth: making money is loud, but managing money is quiet. No one's clapping when you open a savings account, but that's the kind of move that creates freedom. Freedom from anxiety. Freedom from burnout. Freedom from begging. Mastering cash flow is mastering your peace. It's making sure your business feeds you, not just drains you. When you know your numbers, respect your hustle, and plan like a boss, the money starts flowing on your terms. Not by chance, but by choice. Not by panic, but by power.

I know what it's like to make a thousand dollars in one day and still feel broke by the end of the week. I used to think income meant success, but I had to learn that *cash flow* is the real game changer. In my early salon days, the money came fast, walk-ins, appointments, tips, booth rent. But I wasn't tracking anything.

I was making money, not managing it. It wasn't until I started sitting down with a notebook, logging every dollar, that I saw the leaks in my boat. And baby, those leaks were deep. I had to learn to stop romanticizing hustle and start respecting my numbers.

There were seasons I didn't have backup plans, I was the backup. I had employees looking to me, clients counting on me, bills stacked, and no savings. That pressure is a different kind of weight. But it forced me to elevate. I started creating what I call "money rhythms," regular, repeatable ways money could come in, no matter what was happening around me. If nobody walked through the door, I still had books selling. If I needed to slow down physically, my digital classes kept going. That's when I realized: security isn't about how hard you work, it's about how smart you build.

I remember a time after paying all the bills, I had only $37 left for the week, and I sat in my car thinking desperately what else i could do for more money. I was already working seven day a week at the salon. I began questioning how I survived so long with only income from the salon.. I had been blessed but the economy had changed and i could not deny that. Deep down, I knew I wasn't built to quit. So I got up, prayed, designed a $55 special on braids, and passed out fliers like my life depended on it, because it did. That one day brought in $800. I split it, half to bills, half to buy more supplies. That became my formula: flip what you have, invest smart, and keep that flow moving. Cash flow doesn't always start big, sometimes it starts with a faithful $37 and a mindset that refuses to fold.

Boots on the ground foot work is what kept my business afloat. The hair business is unpredictable so i never stopped advertising. Even when I knew i was closing "A New Vision Dreadlock Studio for good. I was still advertising up until a month before we moved to New Mexico. I wanted all the extra money I could get to finance out move to another state.

Now make no mistake I was always excellent at what did. I was a great braider and Dreadlock technician and I trained my staff to be but consistency saved me more than talent ever did. There are many talented people, one that were more educated, more connected and younger. But I show up daily. I stay visible. I offered value and quality, *and I stay available to receive.* That's how I trained my business to keep money moving. Whether I was behind the chair, behind a mic, or behind a laptop to write a new book, I kept my income streams flowing. Not all of them were producing at the same rate, but they were producing. Some were slow. But slow money is still money, and it stacks when you keep showing up with structure.

One of the best moves I ever made was building multiple lanes for my gifts. Braiding was the foundation, but writing added impact. Teaching braiding classes and life coaching added income. Opening a tattoo shop added another level of expression. You don't have to abandon what you started with, you evolve it. You push it to its limits, like squeezing every bit of lemon juice out of a lemon before you toss the hull in the trash. You stretch it. You stack it. Now I'm in a space where my name moves money even before my hands do. That came from branding, integrity, and setting systems in place that serve me even when I need to rest.

What most people miss is that evolution requires courage. It requires you to stop seeing yourself as just one thing. Just a braider. Just an employee. Just a parent. Just a survivor. You are more layered than that. Your gifts were never meant to live in a single lane. When you give yourself permission to expand, you unlock doors you didn't even know were waiting for you. Expansion is not betrayal of your past. It is honoring it.

There comes a moment when staying comfortable becomes more dangerous than trying something new. Comfort will keep you capped. Comfort will keep you dependent. Comfort will whisper that you should be grateful for what you have instead of reaching for what you deserve. But growth requires discomfort. It requires risk. It requires belief in something you cannot fully see yet. That is where legacy is born.

This is your call to stop shrinking your vision to match your current circumstances. Stop thinking in single streams. Stop limiting your income to what your body can physically produce in one day. You are allowed to build in layers. You are allowed to multiply your gifts. You are allowed to earn from your wisdom, your experience, your voice, and your name. That is not arrogance. That is stewardship.

If you wait until you feel ready, you will wait forever. Readiness is built in motion. Confidence is built in execution. Momentum does not come from perfection, it comes from commitment. Start messy. Start unsure. Start small if you must, but start. Because every system you build today becomes protection for tomorrow.

If I could tell the younger me one thing, it would be this: build it like your life depends on it. Use all your energy early on, because some days you will be tired, discouraged, even invisible. But if the foundation is built and the system is strong, the money still moves. That is the freedom I want for you. I want you to stop living in survival mode and start flowing in strategy. Because when you master consistent cash flow, you don't just stay in business, you build a life that works for you, not against you, and that, my love, is wealth on your terms.

11

Working Your Systems

Automation is one of the most powerful wealth tools of this era, and most people still do not fully understand what it really means. When people hear the word automation, they imagine robots, complicated software, or some unreachable level of technical brilliance. They picture something cold and mechanical, far removed from their own lives. But automation is not about technology replacing you. Automation is about systems supporting you. It is about creating pathways that continue working even when you are not physically present.

Automation is the difference between a hustle and a business. Hustle says, "If I don't show up, money stops." Automation says, "Even when I'm resting, something is still moving." That shift alone changes how your body feels. Freedom is not only having money. Freedom is having time. Freedom is being able to step away without fear that everything will collapse behind you.

I learned this lesson slowly, not from a classroom, but from lived experience. When your income is built entirely on skill and service, it is easy to become the machine without realizing it. Your hands become the tool. Your time becomes the inventory. Your energy becomes the engine. At first, that feels empowering. You feel needed. You feel productive. You feel strong. But over time, it becomes exhausting. Because if the only way money enters your life is through constant effort, your nervous system never truly rests.

Automation is how you stop trading your life for income. It is how you move from working hard to working wisely. It allows you to take what you know, what you have lived, and what you have learned, and turn it into systems that generate income repeatedly. That is residual income. That is scalable income. That is income that does not disappear the moment you slow down.

Automation is no longer optional for people who want real financial peace. It is the language of modern wealth. Systems are the new employees. Processes are the new managers. Digital tools are the quiet assistants working in the background. And the most empowering part is this: you do not need to be rich to build automation. You need intention. You need patience. You need the willingness to set something up once so you do not have to keep carrying it forever.

This is where many hardworking people get stuck. They do everything manually. They repeat the same tasks every day. They answer the same questions again and again. They live in reaction mode instead of design mode. They wake up overwhelmed because structure was never created. But structure is not confinement. Structure is freedom. Structure is what allows your life and your business to breathe.

Automation always begins with a mindset shift. You must decide that your time matters. Not just to your family. Not just to your job. Your time matters to your purpose. When you truly believe your hours are sacred, you stop giving them away to tasks that could be systemized. You start asking better questions. You stop asking how much effort something takes and start asking how long it can last.

That one question can change your life. How can I set this up so it runs without me?

When you build systems, you stop relying on mood and motivation. You stop relying on memory. You stop relying on last-minute panic. Systems do not get tired. Systems do not get overwhelmed. Systems do not spiral emotionally. They simply do what they were designed to do, and that reliability is what allows growth to happen.

In this digital era, automation shows up in more forms than most people realize. It can be a book that sells while you sleep. It can be a journal or puzzle book that continues generating income long after creation. It can be an online course that delivers lessons automatically. It can be a membership community that renews month after month. It can be pre-recorded coaching, licensed content, digital downloads, or evergreen resources that remain available without your constant involvement.

Automation is not about removing the personal touch. It is about protecting it. When systems handle repetitive tasks, your creativity stays alive. Your nervous system calms. Your thinking becomes clearer. You show up better because you are no longer stretched thin.

This is especially important for people who have lived in survival mode for a long time. When you are used to scrambling, resting can feel unsafe. Slowing down can feel irresponsible. Automation gently retrains your nervous system. It teaches you that order does not mean loss of control. It means safety. It means predictability. It means peace.

Automation also protects your future self. The version of you who may want to relocate, travel, heal, or simply enjoy life more fully. When you build systems now, you are showing compassion to who you are becoming. You are saying, "I don't want to rebuild everything every season. I want something that can carry me."

There is dignity in automation. It honors the work you already did. It allows your past effort to continue serving you instead of being forgotten once the task is finished. Your wisdom stays active. Your knowledge stays available. Your work stays useful.

This is why people who build wealth focus on systems. They are not necessarily smarter. They simply stopped doing everything by hand. They stopped tying income to exhaustion. They stopped believing struggle was noble. They designed income streams that could continue even when life required them to slow down.

Automation creates consistency, and consistency builds trust. People trust what shows up regularly. People trust what feels organized. People trust what feels stable. Systems make your work feel professional even when you are still growing behind the scenes.

Automation does not remove faith from your work. It honors faith. God is a God of order, and order invites increase. When your systems are aligned, your energy is protected and your creativity expands.

When you automate, you build invisible employees. Systems that collect information, deliver products, follow up, remind, repeat, and support your work quietly in the background. They do not get sick. They do not burn out. They simply work.

In a world where technology connects us instantly, your

presence no longer has to be physical to be powerful. Your message can still circulate. Your income can still flow. Your work can still bless others while you are resting, parenting, healing, or living.

Automation is not about becoming cold or mechanical. It is about becoming free. Free to think. Free to dream. Free to breathe. When you finally create space, your creativity expands. Your ideas sharpen. Your confidence grows. You are no longer drowning in small tasks. You are finally operating from your gift.

If you want to make more money, effort alone will not get you there. Effort is honorable, but effort without strategy becomes struggle. You are not called to struggle forever. You are called to build. You are called to evolve.

Let systems carry what your spirit was never meant to carry alone.

Money responds to structure. Prosperity responds to order. Increase responds to consistency. When you build systems that work without you, money stops feeling chased and starts feeling aligned.

This is not just automation. This is liberation, freedom belongs to the builders.

12

Make it All from Home

Some of the greatest businesses, brands, and movements in history did not begin in boardrooms or corporate offices. They were born in bedrooms, basements, backyards, and kitchen corners. They started with people who were tired, unsure, and still willing to try. I know this because I lived it. I did not wait for perfect conditions. I did not wait for approval. I started where I was, with what I had, and with a decision that I would no longer let fear determine my future. That is the truth no one sells you. You do not need a loan to launch a legacy. You need clarity, courage, and consistency. If you have those three things, you already have more than most.

Your house is not too small. Your voice is not too quiet. Your past is not too messy. You are already equipped. That dining room corner you keep overlooking, that couch, that desk in the hallway, that little space you think does not matter is your office now. The same phone you scroll on is the same phone you can record with, sell from, teach on, and promote with. The same Wi-Fi you use to stream shows is the same Wi-Fi that can power your income. You have been waiting for a sign. This is it. You are the business. You are the brand. You are the product. And now is the perfect time to show up for yourself, even if that means starting right where you are.

I built In59Seconds Publishing Co. from my home, inside my little pink office. I was preparing to move my family to New Mexico and close my salon for good, and I knew I could no longer depend on a single stream of income. For months, I stayed up late watching YouTube videos, teaching myself publishing, formatting, technology, and systems that once intimidated me. It was not easy. Very quickly, I understood why I had paid so much money to the publishing company that released my first three books. There were countless systems to learn. I'm sure I did it wrong fifty times. I was frustrated, overwhelmed, and exhausted more than once, but I refused to quit, and eventually, I got it right. From that point forward, I published my own books and launched my publishing company before ever leaving California.

When I began advertising those new self published books, people started reaching out, asking how they could start their own book journey. They wanted guidance. They wanted help. They wanted what I had taken the time to learn. That was the moment it all made sense. For the first time in my life, I was making money that did not come from my salon. I had been blessed by that business for decades, but I was fifty-six years old and ready for a different season. Income-producing assets were no longer optional. They were necessary.

I know what it feels like to have too many responsibilities and not enough resources. I wrote my first book while braiding hair full time. I printed fliers at the library and cut them by hand. I promoted my work on foot and by faith. I took the little I had and turned it into more, not by luck, but by persistence and refusing to quit. I did not wait for perfect timing. I moved while things were still messy.

The truth is, clarity does not come from thinking. It comes from doing. Momentum is created by action. The moment you decide to move, doors open that you could not see while standing still. In this era, the people who win are the ones who stop consuming and start creating. You have learned enough. You have watched enough. You have waited long enough. There is something inside you that someone else needs, whether it is your story, your skill, your experience, or your wisdom.

This is not about getting rich overnight. This is about stability, peace, and sustainability. It is about designing a life where your income does not depend solely on your physical labor. You have survived long enough. Now it is time to build something that supports you, even when you are tired.

The internet is the new storefront. It is the new stage. It is the new street corner. You can reach the world without leaving your home. If you can teach, write, coach, create, organize, design, speak, or inspire, you can monetize. That thing you think is small is not small. That advice you give away is valuable. That encouragement you offer is currency.

I learned early that branding is not just colors and logos. Branding is energy. When I built Braids By SaBrina and A New Vision Dreadlock Studio, everything was purple. My walls were purple. My fliers were purple. My cards were purple. People associated that color with my work, my excellence, and my consistency. Clients even began bringing me purple gifts because they knew it was my brand. I never changed it, and it worked.

Today, my personal brand is royal blue, navy blue, magenta, and white. Those colors represent balance, strength, creativity, and inclusivity. Men see the blue and feel welcomed. Women see the magenta and feel represented. Consistency built recognition, and recognition built trust. Branding is simply showing up the same way long enough for people to remember you.

Legacy is built from the inside. It begins with mindset. When life knocks you down, it is easy to believe things are impossible. But all things are possible. We are energy. Our thoughts carry frequency. What we consistently think, speak, and believe shapes what shows up in our lives. Gratitude raises you. Fear lowers you. Focus determines direction.

I learned to encourage myself. I learned to shift my energy intentionally. Writing, prayer, music, gratitude, and visualization became tools. When I focused on abundance, opportunities followed. When I believed I was worthy, doors opened. When I stopped waiting and started creating, everything changed.

Your mind is a garden. It grows what you plant. Plant fear and fear will grow. Plant faith and faith will multiply. Visualize the life you want. Feel it. Believe it. Speak it as done. Faith is believing in things unseen as if they already are.

You are not just an entrepreneur. You are a builder. A teacher. A leader. A brand. A legacy in motion. Your story matters. Your experience matters. Your voice matters. Build from where you are. Create from what you know. Launch from your home. Let this be the chapter where you stop hesitating and start building.

Legacy does not begin when you die. It begins the moment you decide to live fully in your purpose. Sit at the table. Open the laptop. Speak. Write. Create. Launch. Action changes everything.

This is not a rehearsal. This is not practice life. This is the moment you stop waiting for permission and start trusting the timing of your own becoming. The world has changed, and for the first time in history, building from home is not a limitation, it is an advantage. You are not late. You are right on time. Staying home is no longer something you have to explain or justify. It is strategy. It is efficiency. It is wisdom. it is power.

You were not born just to survive paycheck to paycheck, managing exhaustion as a lifestyle. You were born to create, to build, to expand, and to leave something meaningful behind. There is a reason your ideas will not leave you alone. There is a reason your spirit keeps nudging you forward. That is not anxiety. That is assignment. That is purpose asking for movement. And the only thing standing between you and the life you want is the decision to begin.

Let this be the year you stop minimizing yourself. Stop down-playing your ability. Stop waiting for confidence to magically appear. Confidence is built by action, not by thinking about action. You do not need to see the entire staircase. You only need to take the next step. When you move, momentum meets you. When you commit, resources show up. When you believe, solutions follow. Everything you need will rise to meet you once you rise to meet yourself.

What makes this moment different is not just personal growth, it is economic reality. The world has changed, and pretending otherwise does not protect anyone. Housing costs have skyrocketed. Interest rates are higher. Groceries cost more. Gas costs more. Insurance costs more. Education costs more. Everything costs more. The economy is quietly but firmly insisting that one stream of income is no longer enough for most families to live with stability, dignity, and peace.

I remember when my first apartment was six hundred dollars a month. That felt expensive at the time, but it was manageable.

Today, our children and grandchildren cannot even find a room for that price. Many of them are working full-time jobs and still cannot afford to live independently. This is not a failure of effort. It is a shift in the system. And when systems change, strategies must change too.

The truth is simple and uncomfortable: the cost of living now requires creativity, adaptability, and multiple income streams. If young adults are not taught how to generate additional income, parents and grandparents will be forced to carry that financial burden longer and longer. Not because they want to, but because survival demands it. Teaching income creation is no longer optional. It is generational responsibility.

Economic shifts do not happen in a vacuum. Global events, policy decisions, inflation, corporate consolidation, and techno-logical disruption have all played a role in reshaping the financial landscape. Jobs that once supported entire households now barely support one person. Pensions are disappearing. Loyalty is no longer rewarded the way it once was. And yet, opportunity has expanded in new directions for those willing to adapt.

This is not about fear. This is about awareness. Awareness gives you options. Awareness allows you to prepare instead of panic. The digital world, remote work, and home-based businesses are not trends, they are structural changes. COVID accelerated what was already coming. Working from home became normalized. Side projects became survival strategies. And when the world reopened, many people realized they never wanted to go back to the old way of living.

What used to be considered "extra" income is now essential income. What used to be called a side hustle is now a safety net. Multiple streams are no longer about luxury. They are about resilience. They are about giving your family options. They are about protecting your future from forces you cannot control.

This is why building from home matters so deeply. It allows flexibility in uncertain times. It allows you to create without asking permission. It allows you to respond to economic shifts instead of being crushed by them. Home is no longer just where you rest. It is where you build. It is where you strategize. It is where legacy begins.

You do not need a perfect office, a fancy logo, or a team of ten to begin. You need a decision. You need a moment where you stop waiting for permission and you start honoring the pressure you have been feeling inside. That pressure is not meant to crush you. It is meant to push you into the version of yourself that no longer settles, no longer hesitates, no longer says "one day." One day is not a date on the calendar. One day is a mindset. This your year to change it.

I want you to understand something deeply personal: I didn't start with some big building or some "perfect setup." I started from home. From my computer. From my cute little pink computer desk in my house. I built In 59 Seconds Publishing Company with faith in one hand and determination in the other. I started with what I had, where I was, and I refused to talk myself out of my own future. That is what real builders do. They don't wait for life to get quiet. They build while life is still loud.

And if I can do it, you can do it too. I am not saying that like a motivational quote. I am saying it as a living testimony. You can create income from home. You can create a business from home. You can create a brand from home. You can create your first stream of residual income from the same place you cry, pray, cook, clean, raise babies, and recover from the hard seasons. Your home is not holding you back. Your home can become your launchpad.

Because money is not only something you chase. It is something you learn to create. It is something you learn to attract through value, through skill, through consistency, and through courage. You don't need to be famous. You don't need to be perfect. You just need to be willing. Willing to learn. Willing to try. Willing to show up on the days you feel unsure. Willing to keep going when nobody claps at the beginning. The beginning is usually lonely, but it is still holy.

Some of you have been surviving for so long that building feels selfish. It is not. It is stewardship. It is protection. It is you deciding that struggle will not be the family tradition you pass down. It is you deciding that your children will not only inherit your love, they will inherit your example. They will remember the year you got serious. They will remember the year you stopped saying "I can't" and started saying "watch me." They will remember that you built something out of nothing but faith and focus.

This is for the person who feels behind. For the person who feels embarrassed that they're starting over. For the person who feels like life took too much from them already. Listen to me: starting over is not a sentence. It is a strategy. It is proof that you still have fight in you. You are not late. You are not forgotten. You are not disqualified. You are being rebuilt from the inside, and that kind of foundation lasts.

So when you wake each day, do not wake up to fear. Wake up to intention. Wake up to your own voice saying, "This year, I build." Wake up to the mindset that says, "I can learn what I don't know." Wake up to the belief that says, "God didn't place this vision in me to tease me." Wake up and treat your dream like an assignment, not a fantasy. Even if it's only one hour a day, even if it's after work, even if it's while the kids are sleeping, even if it's from a tiny desk in the corner of your living room, it still counts. It still changes your life.

You don't have to be fearless. You just have to be faithful. Faith is not loud. Faith is consistent. Faith is you showing up again after yesterday didn't go the way you wanted. Faith is you sending the email. Posting the product. Making the phone call. Writing the first page. Launching the first offer. Learning the skill. Building the website. Telling yourself the truth until your emotions catch up. Faith looks like movement.

When doubt tries to talk you out of it, remember this: you were not created to be a spectator in your own life. You were created to create. To build. To provide. To expand. To leave something behind that proves you were here and you believed in what God placed inside you. This is your legacy season. Not someday. Now. And it can start from home.

So take one more breath, and let it be the breath of a builder. The kind of builder who doesn't wait for the world to change, because she knows she can change her world. The kind of builder who doesn't wait for permission, because he knows purpose is permission. The kind of builder who looks at each day and says, "This is my year to rise and shine." You are ready. You are more than worthy. You are needed by the world. Now go build what was placed inside you.

About the Author

SaBrina Fisher Reece writes self-help books rooted in emotional healing, personal growth, and spiritual awareness. Her work blends lived experience with motivational insight, often exploring themes of balance, resilience, self-mastery, and the unseen forces that shape our thoughts and behaviors. Drawing from both practical reflection and metaphysical concepts, her writing encourages readers to develop greater self-awareness, reconnect with their inner strength, and create more intentional, aligned lives.

Also by SaBrina Fisher Reece

For more than twenty-six years, she built one of the most influential braiding salons and schools in Los Angeles, **Braids By SaBrina**, earning statewide recognition as *"The Braid Queen."* Her success was self-made, built through discipline, resilience, and vision, often without consistent support or validation from others.

Shaped by early abandonment, profound loss, and hard-earned self-trust, SaBrina's life journey led her to explore emotional healing, spiritual alignment, and self-mastery. Today, she is an author, speaker, and guide dedicated to helping others develop inner balance, confidence, and emotional strength.

She is the author of numerous self-help and transformational works, including *My Spiritual Smile*, *Your Mind Is Magic*, *Perfectly Positive*, *Spiritual Balance*, *Living Life on a Higher Frequency*, *Become Your Own Cheerleader*, *Kicking Depression in the Butt*, *Self Sabotage*, *How to Get Exactly What You Want From God*, When I Say "I Am"

PROFOUND

Introduction to the Profound Series

This series was not written to convince you of anything.

It was written to remind you of something.

For most of my life, I searched for answers the same way many people do. I looked outward. I prayed, studied, worked, endured, and tried to become better by force. I believed growth meant effort alone and that transformation required suffering. I was taught, as many of us are, what to believe, what to question, and what to avoid.

What I did not realize at the time was that I was not missing faith.

I was missing understanding.

The *Profound Series* was born from a deeply personal journey of self-discovery, healing, and expansion. It is the result of decades of reading ancient texts, studying metaphysical teachings, reflecting on spiritual principles, and most importantly, applying this wisdom in real life. This series is not meant to replace religion, tradition, or belief systems. It is meant to widen the lens.

Religion offers structure, community, and devotion. Ancient wisdom offers context, depth, and responsibility. Together, they reveal something powerful: that you are not separate from the divine, and you were never meant to live disconnected from your inner power.

This series exists because I discovered that much of what we are seeking has already been known for centuries. Long before modern psychology, neuroscience, or self-help, ancient philosophers, mystics, teachers, and spiritual scholars understood the relationship between thought, emotion, consciousness, and reality. They understood that the mind is creative, that belief shapes experience, and that life responds to awareness.

The first book, **Profound**, is about remembering. It is about gathering ancient wisdom and recognizing truths that may feel familiar even if you are encountering them for the first time. This is the awakening stage. The moment when something inside you says, "There is more."

The second book, **Activate**, is about embodiment. Knowledge alone does not change a life. It must be practiced. This book moves wisdom from the intellect into daily living. It teaches you how to tap into the divine energy within you and apply what you have learned in practical, grounded ways.

The third book, **Think**, is about mastery of the mind. Thought is not passive. It is creative. This book guides you in becoming aware of your inner dialogue, understanding how thoughts shape experience, and learning how to consciously direct the mental patterns that influence your life.

The fourth book, **Live**, is about integration. This is where knowledge, practice, and awareness become who you are. You no longer strive to be aligned. You live aligned. You move through the world with clarity, compassion, and confidence, embodying the wisdom you have gained.

Together, these four books form a complete journey.

Awakening. Activation. Mastery. Expression.

This is not a quick fix. It is not spiritual bypassing. It is not about perfection. It is about responsibility. Responsibility for your thoughts. Responsibility for your emotional state. Responsibility for the energy you bring into the world.

The world does not need more information. It needs more

conscious people. People who are self-aware. People who understand cause and effect at the level of thought and emotion. People who can pause, reflect, and respond instead of react. People who live from inner alignment rather than fear.

You were never meant to live small, disconnected, or power-less. You were meant to participate in your own evolution.

This series is an invitation. Not to abandon what you believe, but to expand it. Not to follow me, but to follow your own inner knowing. Not to search endlessly outside yourself, but to reconnect with what has always been within you.

If you are reading this, you are ready.

Ready to remember.

Ready to activate.

Ready to master your mind.

Ready to live fully.

Welcome to the journey.

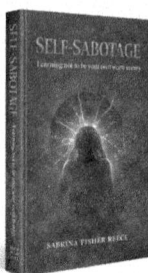

Self-Sabotage

Self-Sabotage: Learning Not to Be Your Own Worst Enemy explores the emotional and psychological patterns that cause individuals to unknowingly work against their own growth, happiness, and healing. Drawing from lived experience, emotional awareness, and spiritual insight, SaBrina Fisher Reece examines how trauma, fear, and unresolved pain often manifest as self-defeating thoughts and behaviors.

Rather than approaching self-sabotage through judgment or blame, this book reframes it as a learned survival response that can be unlearned through awareness, compassion, and intentional change. Readers are guided to recognize destructive cycles, understand their emotional roots, and begin developing a healthier relationship with themselves.

This book is designed for readers seeking personal growth, emotional healing, and greater self-understanding. It offers practical insight into breaking harmful patterns and reclaiming inner balance, making it a valuable resource for anyone ready to stop standing in their own way and move forward with clarity and confidence.

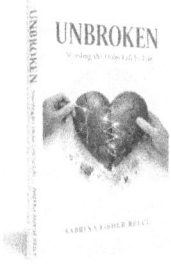

Unbroken

Unbroken: Mending the Holes Left by Life is a self-help and personal growth book that explores emotional healing after trauma, abandonment, and loss. Drawing from lived experience and spiritual insight, SaBrina Fisher Reece introduces the concept of "holes" formed by unresolved pain and explains how these wounds influence thoughts, behaviors, and relationships.

This book guides readers toward greater self-awareness, emotional balance, and inner healing by addressing the mind's role in recovery and the importance of compassion, forgiveness, and intentional thought patterns. *Unbroken* offers a reflective and empowering approach to healing, helping readers understand their past without being controlled by it.

Designed for individuals seeking emotional growth and spiritual grounding, *Unbroken* provides insight into reclaiming wholeness and learning how to live with strength, clarity, and self-love after life's most difficult experiences.

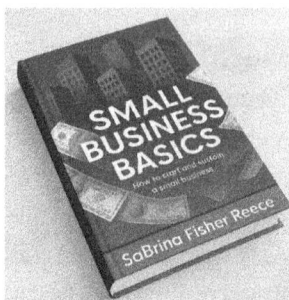

Small Business Basics:

Small Business Basics: How to Start and Sustain a Small Business is a powerful, practical guide for new and aspiring entrepreneurs from SaBrina Fisher Reece-an accomplished businesswoman who has successfully built, managed, and sustained multiple thriving enterprises in Los Angeles for over 30 years. Drawing from her experience as the sole proprietor of the iconic Braids By SaBrina, Inked 4 Life Tattoo Studio, and A New Vision Dreadlock Studio.

In this book SaBrina shares the real-world wisdom, essential tools, and spiritual principles that helped her turn personal adversity into a legacy of entrepreneurial success.

This book teaches readers how to navigate the do's and dont's of small business ownership, master strategic advertising, attract loyal customers, negotiate with confidence, and build a business rooted in both profit and purpose. More than a manual, it is a motivational roadmap for perseverance, faith, and financial empowerment-from a woman who has lived it, built it, and sustained.

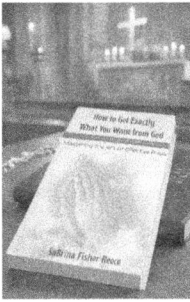

How to Get Exactly What You Want From God

How to Get Exactly What You Want From God: Mastering the Art of Effective prayer: shows you how to pray with results. Inside, you'll learn how to make specific requests, build the faith needed to sustain them, and match your thoughts and emotions to the outcome you want. SaBrina teaches you how to interrupt negative self-talk, eliminate doubt, and step into a mindset that attracts divine answers quickly and clearly. This is your guide to intentional prayer, spiritual alignment, and receiving blessings without hesitation.

What if prayer was never meant to be begging, pleading or waiting in doubt - but instead a powerful alignment with what God has already promised you?

In this amazing book *SaBrina Fisher Reece* dismantles the myths around ineffective prayer and exposes the spiritual authority each believer already possesses. Blending deep spiritual wisdom, real life testimonies of divine intervention, and the practical mindset of a seasoned entrepreneur. SaBrina teaches readers how to pray with confidence, clarity, gratitude and expectation, so they can finally see there hearts desires appear in real time.

Through powerful personal stories of protection, provision, survival and miraculous alignment, SaBrina reveals that prayer becomes effective when belief replaces fear and faith replaces uncertainty. The Kingdom of Heaven is already within you. This book is not about religion as routine - it is about relationship, authority and conscious co-creation with God.

In this book you will learn:

. Eliminate doubt from your prayer

. Speak with spiritual authority and conscious intention

. Align your thoughts, emotions and actions with your prayers

. Recognize Divine intervention in your life

. Trust God's timing without losing hope

This is not a book about hoping and wishing.

This is a book about knowing and trusting that "It Already Done!"

Effective prayer doesn't wonder if God will move - it prepares your life for when He does

www.ingramcontent.com/pod-product-compliance
Lightning Source LLC
Chambersburg PA
CBHW070943210326
41520CB00021B/7036